D1707928

DISCARDED

The Planets

Carmel Reilly

Marshall Cavendish
Benchmark
New York

This edition first published in 2012 in the United States of America by
Marshall Cavendish Benchmark
An imprint of Marshall Cavendish Corporation

All rights reserved.

No part of this publication may be reproduced, stored in a retrieval system or transmitted, in any form or by any means, electronic, mechanical, photocopying, recording, or otherwise, without the prior permission of the copyright owner. Request for permission should be addressed to the Publisher, Marshall Cavendish Corporation, 99 White Plains Road, Tarrytown, NY 10591. Tel: (914) 332-8888, fax: (914) 332-1888.

Website: www.marshallcavendish.us

This publication represents the opinions and views of the author based on Carmel Reilly's personal experience, knowledge, and research. The information in this book serves as a general guide only. The author and publisher have used their best efforts in preparing this book and disclaim liability rising directly and indirectly from the use and application of this book.

Other Marshall Cavendish Offices: Marshall Cavendish International (Asia) Private Limited, 1 New Industrial Road, Singapore 536196 • Marshall Cavendish International (Thailand) Co Ltd. 253 Asoke, 12th Flr, Sukhumvit 21 Road, Klongtoey Nua, Wattana, Bangkok 10110, Thailand • Marshall Cavendish (Malaysia) Sdn Bhd, Times Subang, Lot 46, Subang Hi-Tech Industrial Park, Batu Tiga, 40000 Shah Alam, Selangor Darul Ehsan, Malaysia

Marshall Cavendish is a trademark of Times Publishing Limited

All websites were available and accurate when this book was sent to press.

Library of Congress Cataloging-in-Publication Data

Reilly, Carmel, 1957-
  The planets / Carmel Reilly.
      p. cm. — (Sky watching)
  Includes index.
  Summary: "Provides scientific information about the planets"—Provided by publisher.
  ISBN 978-1-60870-582-5
  1. Planets—Juvenile literature. 2. Astronomy—Observers' manuals—Juvenile literature. I. Title.
  QB602.R45 2012
  523.4—dc22
                              2010044017

Publisher: Carmel Heron
Commissioning Editor: Niki Horin
Managing Editor: Vanessa Lanaway
Project Editor: Tim Clarke
Editor: Paige Amor
Proofreader: Helena Newton
Designer: Polar Design
Page layout: Romy Pearse
Photo Researcher: Legendimages
Illustrator: Adrian Hogan
Production Controller: Vanessa Johnson

Printed in China

Acknowledgments

The author and publisher are grateful to the following for permission to reproduce copyright material:

Front cover photograph: The planet Mars shining in the night sky above Taftan volcano on the border of Iran and Pakistan courtesy of Photolibrary/Science Photo Library/Babk Tafreshi.

Photographs courtesy of: Calvin J Hamilton/Solar Views, **10** (all), **11** (all); iStockphoto/Martin Adams, **18**, /Mike Sonnenberg, **5** (bottom), /Sergii Tsololo, border element throughout; NASA, **12**; NASA, painting by Donald E. Davis, **28**; NASA and The Hubble Heritage Team (STScI/AURA) [R.G. French (Wellesley College), J. Cuzzi (NASA/Ames), L. Dones (SwRI), and J. Lissauer (NASA/Ames)], **20**; NASA/Johns Hopkins University Applied Physics Laboratory/Carnegie Institution of Washington, **13**, /JPL, **14**, **19**, **21**, /JPL/ESA, **27**, /Lunar and Planetary Laboratory, **5** (top); Photolibrary/Science Photo Library, **22**, /Science Photo Library RF, **16**, **23**, /Science Photo Library/John Sanford, **8**, /Science Photo Library/Babk Tafreshi, **1**.

While every care has been taken to trace and acknowledge copyright, the publisher tenders their apologies for any accidental infringement where copyright has proved untraceable. They would be pleased to come to a suitable arrangement with the rightful owner in each case.

Please Note
At the time of printing, the Internet addresses appearing in this book were correct. Owing to the dynamic nature of the Internet, however, we cannot guarantee that all these addresses will remain correct.

Contents

Glossary Words

Words that are printed in **bold** are explained in the glossary on page 31.

What Does It Mean?

Words that are within a **box** are explained in the "What Does It Mean?" panel at the bottom of the page.

SKY WATCHING

When we sky watch, we look at everything above Earth. This includes what is in Earth's **atmosphere** and the objects we can see beyond it, in space .

Why Do We Sky Watch?

Sky watching helps us understand more about Earth's place in space. Earth is our home. It is also a planet that is part of a space neighborhood called the **solar system**. When we sky watch we learn about Earth, and our neighbors inside and outside the solar system.

What Objects Are in the Sky?

There are thousands of objects in the sky above Earth. These are Earth's neighbors— the Sun, the Moon, planets, stars, and flying space rocks (**comets**, **asteroids**, and **meteoroids**). Some can be seen at night and others can be seen during the day. Although some are visible with the human eye, all objects must be viewed through a telescope to be seen more clearly.

When and How Can We See Objects in the Sky?				
Object in the Sky	Visible with Only the Human Eye 👁	Visible Only through a Telescope 🔦	Visible during the Day ☀	Visible at Night 🌙
Earth's Atmosphere	✗	✗	✗	✗
Sun	✓ (Do not view directly)	✗ (View only with a special telescope)	✓	✗
Moon	✓	✗	Sometimes	✓
Planets	Sometimes	Sometimes	Sometimes	✓
Stars	Sometimes	Sometimes	✗	✓
Comets	Sometimes	Sometimes	✗	✓
Asteroids	Sometimes	Sometimes	✗	✓
Meteoroids	Sometimes	Sometimes	✗	✓

WHAT DOES IT MEAN **space** The area in which the solar system, stars, and galaxies exist, also known as the universe.

THE PLANETS

The planets are space objects we can see in the night sky. Most are visible with the human eye. However, some can only be seen through a telescope. The planets in our solar system are Mercury, Venus, Earth, Mars, Jupiter, Saturn, Uranus, and Neptune.

Planet Watching

People have always watched the planets. Since the invention of telescopes 500 years ago, we have been able to see them more clearly. Now, because of space exploration, we have found out even more about the planets. Today people now know what they are made of, what their atmospheres are like, and how they affect Earth.

Sky watching can be done during the day or night, with or without a telescope. Just look up!

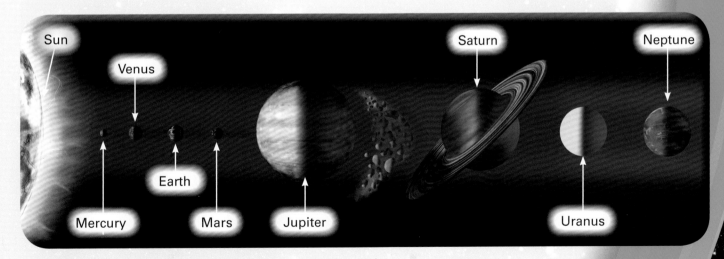

Sun   Venus   Earth   Saturn   Neptune   Mercury   Mars   Jupiter   Uranus

The planets are some of our closest neighbors in space. This diagram shows the approximate relative sizes of the Sun and the planets. The distances between them are not to scale.

WHAT ARE THE PLANETS?

The planets formed after the Sun was born, billions of years ago. They are huge balls made of rock or **gas** that [orbit] the Sun.

The Planets Were Formed from Leftover Gas and Dust

The solar system formed from a huge, spinning cloud of gas and dust called a **nebula**. The Sun was born from this nebula about 4.7 billion years ago. About 4.6 billion years ago, [gravity] slowly brought the leftover gas and dust circling the Sun together, to form the planets.

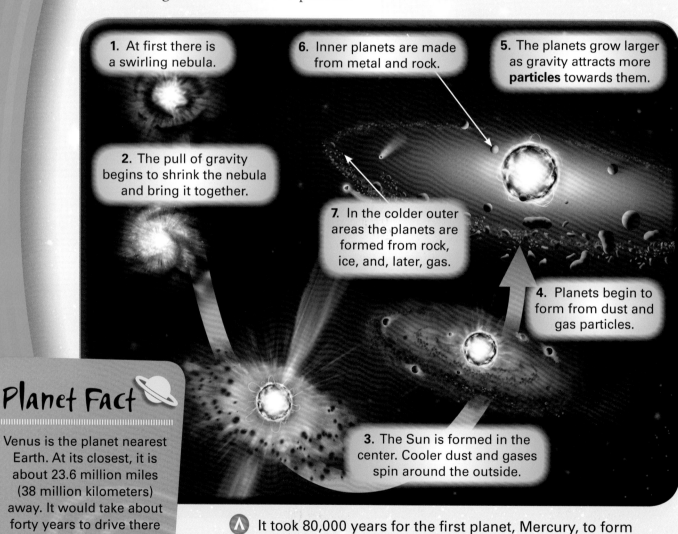

1. At first there is a swirling nebula.

6. Inner planets are made from metal and rock.

5. The planets grow larger as gravity attracts more **particles** towards them.

2. The pull of gravity begins to shrink the nebula and bring it together.

7. In the colder outer areas the planets are formed from rock, ice, and, later, gas.

4. Planets begin to form from dust and gas particles.

3. The Sun is formed in the center. Cooler dust and gases spin around the outside.

It took 80,000 years for the first planet, Mercury, to form from the particles of gas and dust orbiting around the Sun.

Planet Fact

Venus is the planet nearest Earth. At its closest, it is about 23.6 million miles (38 million kilometers) away. It would take about forty years to drive there from Earth in a car.

WHAT DOES IT MEAN

orbit To travel around another, larger space object.

gravity The force that attracts all objects toward each other.

The Planets Are Balls of Rock and Gas that Orbit the Sun

Besides Earth, there are seven planets that orbit the Sun. Earth and three other inner planets, Mercury, Venus, and Mars, are made up mostly of rock. Jupiter, Saturn, Uranus, and Neptune orbit farther from the Sun. They are made up mostly of gases.

The Sun's Gravity Keeps the Planets in Orbit

The planets orbit the Sun because its gravity pulls on them as they move through space. The Sun's **gravitational pull** keeps the planets on the same orbital paths and stops them from flying off into space.

FAMOUS SKY WATCHERS

Johannes Kepler, a German astronomer, discovered that the planets' orbits are elliptical, or oval-shaped. He found that the farther away a planet is from the Sun, the slower its speed. He also discovered that the size of a planet affects the length of its orbit.

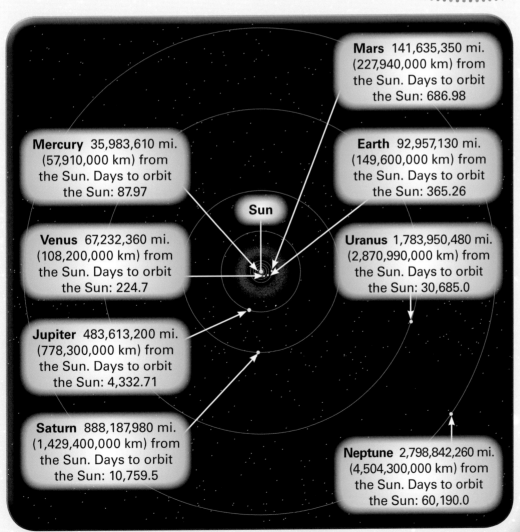

Mars 141,635,350 mi. (227,940,000 km) from the Sun. Days to orbit the Sun: 686.98

Mercury 35,983,610 mi. (57,910,000 km) from the Sun. Days to orbit the Sun: 87.97

Earth 92,957,130 mi. (149,600,000 km) from the Sun. Days to orbit the Sun: 365.26

Sun

Venus 67,232,360 mi. (108,200,000 km) from the Sun. Days to orbit the Sun: 224.7

Uranus 1,783,950,480 mi. (2,870,990,000 km) from the Sun. Days to orbit the Sun: 30,685.0

Jupiter 483,613,200 mi. (778,300,000 km) from the Sun. Days to orbit the Sun: 4,332.71

Saturn 888,187,980 mi. (1,429,400,000 km) from the Sun. Days to orbit the Sun: 10,759.5

Neptune 2,798,842,260 mi. (4,504,300,000 km) from the Sun. Days to orbit the Sun: 60,190.0

Planets that are far away from the Sun take much longer to complete their orbit than planets that are close.

WHAT DO THE PLANETS LOOK LIKE FROM EARTH?

Five planets can be seen from Earth with the human eye. They look like small points of light in the night sky. The other two planets can only be seen through a telescope. None of the planets stay in the same place in the sky.

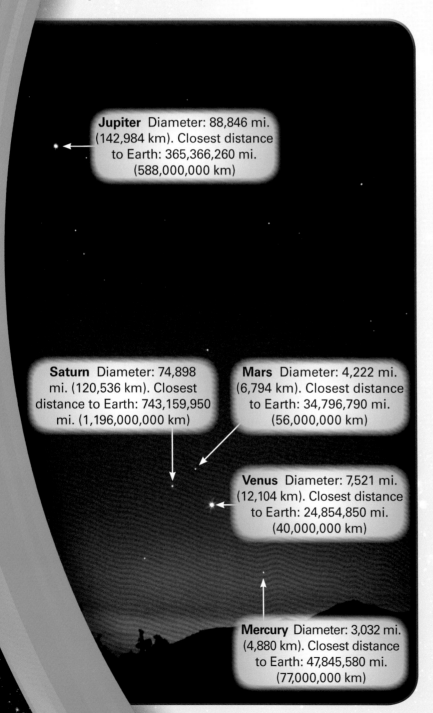

Jupiter Diameter: 88,846 mi. (142,984 km). Closest distance to Earth: 365,366,260 mi. (588,000,000 km)

Saturn Diameter: 74,898 mi. (120,536 km). Closest distance to Earth: 743,159,950 mi. (1,196,000,000 km)

Mars Diameter: 4,222 mi. (6,794 km). Closest distance to Earth: 34,796,790 mi. (56,000,000 km)

Venus Diameter: 7,521 mi. (12,104 km). Closest distance to Earth: 24,854,850 mi. (40,000,000 km)

Mercury Diameter: 3,032 mi. (4,880 km). Closest distance to Earth: 47,845,580 mi. (77,000,000 km)

The Planets Look Like Bright Lights in the Sky

Mercury, Venus, Mars, Jupiter and Saturn can all be seen from Earth with the human eye. These planets seem to shine like stars but they do not "twinkle" like stars. This is because stars make their own light, while the planets just reflect the light of the Sun. Stars twinkle because their light comes from a long way away and it is changed when it enters the Earth's atmosphere. The light from planets is closer and steadier.

How bright the planets appear in the sky depends on how far away they are from Earth and how large they are.

The Planets Move through the Sky

While the stars stay in the same place in the sky each night, the planets change position. Different planets can be seen in the sky at different times of the year. They also move very slowly across the sky when they are visible.

Planet Fact

The word "planet" comes from the Ancient Greek word *plenetes*, which means wanderer. The Ancient Greeks were sky watchers and many of the names for the planets and the stars come from them.

Venus
3rd month

Venus
1st month

Venus
6th month

This diagram illustrates the movement of Venus across the night sky over a period of six months.

WHAT ARE THE PLANETS MADE OF?

From Earth, we cannot tell what is inside the planets. Scientists gather information about the planets using telescopes, and from space exploration. They know that the planets close to the Sun are mostly made of rock. Those farther away are mostly made of gas.

The Closest Planets Are Rocky

Rocky planets formed in the area closest to the Sun. This is because only metal and rock were able to stand the heat in this part of the solar system. All of the planets that formed there are made up of a metal **core**, with a **mantle**, and a **crust** of rock. The rocky planets are Mercury, Mars, Venus, and Earth.

> The rocky planets are alike, but Mercury has the largest metal core and the smallest mantle.

Mercury

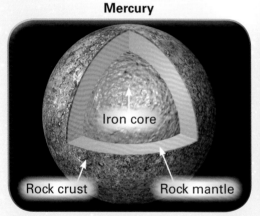

Iron core

Rock crust — Rock mantle

Mars

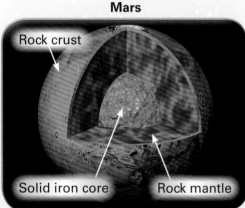

Rock crust

Solid iron core — Rock mantle

Venus

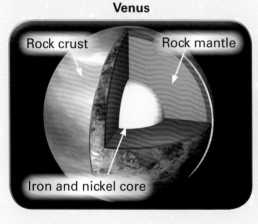

Rock crust — Rock mantle

Iron and nickel core

Earth

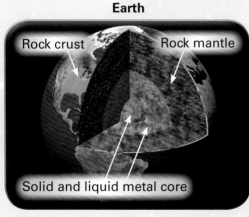

Rock crust — Rock mantle

Solid and liquid metal core

WHAT DOES IT MEAN

core The center of a star, planet, or moon.

mantle The middle layer of a planet or moon, between the crust and the core.

crust The outside layer of a planet or moon.

The Farthest Planets Are Gas Giants

The planets that are known as gas giants are Jupiter, Saturn, Uranus, and Neptune. They all have cores made of rock. The mantles of Jupiter and Saturn are made from the gases **hydrogen** and **helium**. The mantles of Uranus and Neptune are made from **methane**, **ammonia**, and ice. They all have an outer layer of gas that blends into the atmosphere.

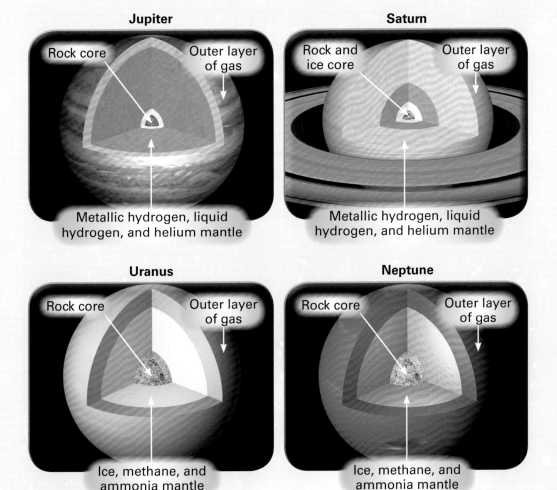

Jupiter

Rock core

Outer layer of gas

Metallic hydrogen, liquid hydrogen, and helium mantle

Saturn

Rock and ice core

Outer layer of gas

Metallic hydrogen, liquid hydrogen, and helium mantle

Uranus

Rock core

Outer layer of gas

Ice, methane, and ammonia mantle

Neptune

Rock core

Outer layer of gas

Ice, methane, and ammonia mantle

⋀ The gas giants have solid cores that are surrounded by different kinds of gases.

FAMOUS SKY WATCHERS

The National Aeronautics and Space Administration (NASA) is the government space agency. In 1979, NASA's space probe *Voyager 1* went to Jupiter and Saturn. In 1989, *Voyager 2* flew past Uranus and Saturn.

WHAT ARE CONDITIONS LIKE ON AND AROUND THE ROCKY PLANETS?

Conditions vary a great deal on the rocky planets. Earth has plenty of water and the right kind of atmosphere to support life. However, the other three rocky planets are dry, harsh, and lifeless.

Earth is the Blue Planet

When space exploration began, people were finally able to see the Earth. Photos taken by space satellites show Earth as a blue planet, wrapped in a swirl of white clouds. It is orbited by one moon.

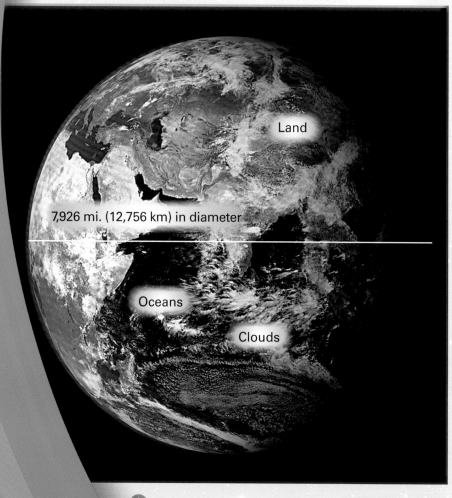

Land

7,926 mi. (12,756 km) in diameter

Oceans

Clouds

Earth's Surface Is Covered in Water

Earth's blue color when seen from space comes from its oceans. They cover about 75 percent of the planet's surface. Having water on Earth has helped life to develop. It also helps keep temperatures even.

Earth's Atmosphere Gives Life

Earth's atmosphere is a blanket of gases that lies around the surface of the planet. It protects people from the harmful rays of the Sun. It also provides all living things with air to breathe and keeps Earth at an even temperature.

Λ Earth is the only planet in our solar system that is home to plant and animal life.

Mercury Is Dusty and Dry

Mercury is the planet closest to the Sun. It is a dusty, lifeless place with extreme temperatures and a thin atmosphere. In the 1970s, space probes flew past Mercury and sent images back to Earth.

Mercury's Surface Is Dry

Mercury's surface is rough, dry, dusty, and waterless. It has many large **plains**, some mountain ranges, and **craters** that were caused by impacts from space objects.

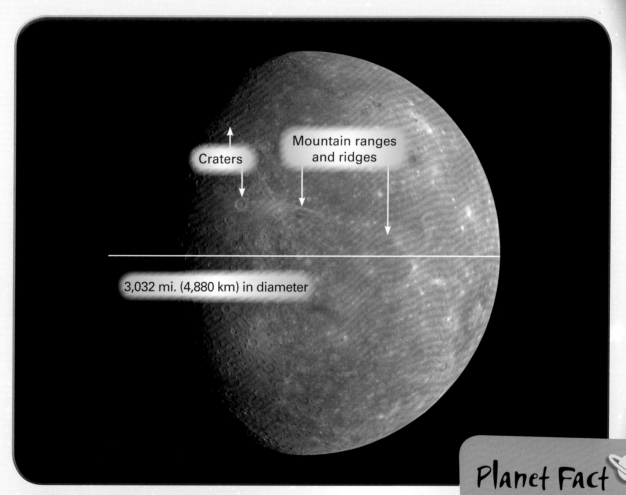

Craters

Mountain ranges and ridges

3,032 mi. (4,880 km) in diameter

More than half the surface of Mercury is covered with impact craters.

Mercury Has a Thin Atmosphere

Mercury has a very thin atmosphere. This is mostly because it does not have enough gravity to keep gases close to its surface. Temperatures on Mercury are extreme because of its thin atmosphere.

Planet Fact

Temperatures on the surface of Mercury range from -292°F (-180°C) to as high as 842°F (450°C). The average temperature of the planet is about seven times higher than on Earth.

Venus Is Dry and Volcanic

Venus is a ball of rock, almost the same size as Earth. It has a thick, hot atmosphere and is covered in volcanoes. Since 1969, scientists have used **radar** to look more closely at Venus.

Venus's Surface Is Volcanic

The surface of Venus is dry, rocky, and volcanic. More than three-quarters of Venus's surface is made up of plains that were formed by **lava** from volcanoes. These plains are dotted with craters from space object impacts. There are also large **highlands** and mountain regions.

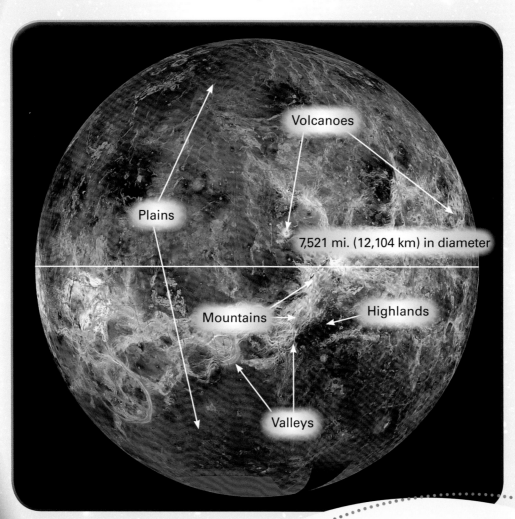

Volcanoes

Plains

7,521 mi. (12,104 km) in diameter

Mountains

Highlands

Valleys

Highland areas make up about 20 percent of Venus's surface. They are about 2.5 to 3.1 mi. (4–5 km) higher than the plains.

FAMOUS SKY WATCHERS

Space probes are used to find out as much as possible about Venus's atmosphere and clouds. In 1970, the Russian probe *Venera 7* was the first probe to reach Venus and send information back to Earth. The European Space Agency's *Venus Express* probe has been orbiting Venus since 2006.

Venus's Atmosphere Is Thick and Poisonous

Venus has a thick, poisonous atmosphere that stretches 50 mi. (80 km) into space. A layer of this atmosphere is made of thick cloud. It contains dust and acid that comes from the volcanoes below. This cloud makes Venus dark and gloomy. It also keeps the heat from the Sun trapped on the surface. This makes the planet very hot.

V Venus's cloudy atmosphere creates a greenhouse effect, keeping the heat from the Sun close to the planet's surface.

Planet Fact

Venus has the hottest atmosphere of any planet in the solar system. Its thick atmosphere keeps temperatures at 867°F (464°C). This is about eighteen times hotter than a warm day on Earth.

Sunlight

Most sunlight is reflected away by the clouds.

Cloud cover stretches from about 25 mi. (40 km) to about 43 mi. (70 km) above the surface.

Carbon dioxide in the atmosphere holds heat.

20% of sunlight reaches the surface of Venus

Heat cannot escape into space.

Mars Is Dusty and Cold

Mars is about half the size of Earth. It is dusty, cold, and dry, with a thin atmosphere. It is orbited by two moons. We have learned about Mars from the space probes that have flown past or landed there.

The Surface of Mars Is Dry and Red

Mars is dry, dusty, and red colored. Large plains can be found in the northern part of the planet. Craters dot the highlands in the south. There are many extinct volcanoes and canyons around the **equator** of Mars. There is ice at the north and south poles.

Mars has the  biggest volcano and the biggest canyon in the solar system. Olympus Mons is the largest volcano and Valles Marineris is the largest known canyon.

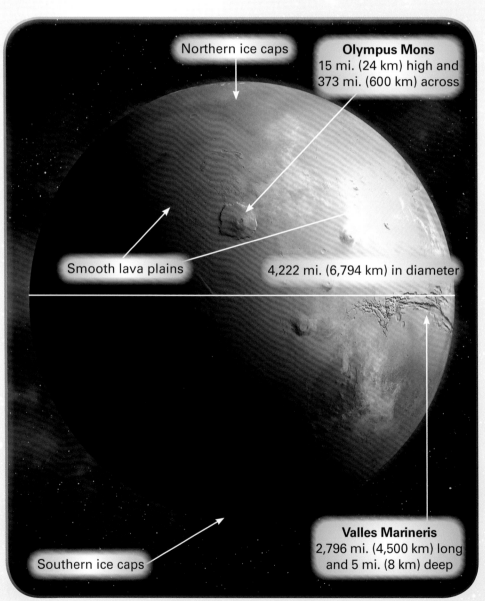

Northern ice caps

Olympus Mons
15 mi. (24 km) high and 373 mi. (600 km) across

Smooth lava plains

4,222 mi. (6,794 km) in diameter

Southern ice caps

Valles Marineris
2,796 mi. (4,500 km) long and 5 mi. (8 km) deep

Planet Fact

Mars was named after the Roman god of war because of its red appearance. Its color comes from the iron oxide (rust) that is found across its surface.

WHAT DOES IT MEAN

equator An imaginary line around the middle or widest part of a round space object, such as a star or planet.

The Atmosphere of Mars Is Thin and Dry

Mars has a thin, dry atmosphere that looks pink because it carries red dust from the planet's surface. It is a cold place, with an average temperature of -81°F (-63°C). Up to one-third of its atmosphere can be frozen at any time. It does not rain on Mars, but it is very windy.

Mars Has Two Moons

Mars is orbited by two moons, called Phobos and Deimos. Astronomers believe the moons were once asteroids that were caught by the gravity on Mars billions of years ago.

V Phobos is slowly being pulled closer to Mars by the planet's gravity. One day it could crash into Mars.

Phobos
Width: 17 mi. (27 km)
Time taken to orbit Mars: 7 hours and 39 minutes
Average distance from Mars: 14,602 mi. (23,500 km)

Deimos
Width: 10 mi. (16 km)
Time taken to orbit Mars: 30 hours and 20 minutes
Average distance from Mars: 5,841 mi. (9,400 km)

WHAT ARE CONDITIONS LIKE ON AND AROUND THE GAS GIANTS?

Conditions on the gas giants are very different from those of Earth. They do not have a solid crust and their outer layers of gas blend into their atmospheres.

Jupiter Is Surrounded by Rings and Moons

Jupiter is the largest planet in our solar system. It is mostly gas and has no solid surface. Jupiter is surrounded by dusty rings and is orbited by sixty-two moons. A space probe orbited Jupiter from 1995 to 2003 and sent information to Earth.

Jupiter Does Not Have a Crust

Instead of a crust, Jupiter has an outer layer that is 621 mi. (1,000 km) thick. This layer is made up of the gases hydrogen and helium. The temperature of this layer is about -166°F (-110°C).

Bands of sulfur clouds lie across the surface.

-166°F (-110°C) on the surface

88,846 mi. (142,984 km) in diameter

Planet Fact

Although the surface of Jupiter is cold, its core is thought to be about 54,032°F (30,000°C). Jupiter is slowly shrinking in size, and as it shrinks, it gives off energy in the form of heat.

∧ The light and dark bands that can be seen on Jupiter are clouds that lie just above its surface.

Jupiter's Atmosphere Creates Huge Storms

Jupiter's atmosphere is a blanket of cloud that is 621 mi. (1,000 km) thick. It is made up of ice, water, and ammonia. Wind in Jupiter's atmosphere creates storms. Some of these are so huge that they can be seen through a telescope from Earth.

Jupiter Is Surrounded by Rings

Jupiter's rings are made of tiny dust particles that have gone into orbit around the planet. The dust comes from space objects that have crashed into Jupiter's moons.

Jupiter Is Surrounded by Many Moons

Jupiter is orbited by sixty-two moons. Ganymede is Jupiter's largest moon. It is the largest moon in the solar system. It is bigger than the planet Mercury.

V Jupiter and its four planet-size moons were photographed by space probe *Voyager 1* and made into this collage. They are not shown to scale but are in their relative positions.

FAMOUS SKY WATCHERS

Simon Marius, a German astronomer, was the first to see Jupiter's four largest Moons in 1610. He named them Ganymede, Callisto, Io, and Europa after characters from Ancient Greek myths.

Jupiter

Io

Europa

Ganymede

Callisto

Saturn Is Cloudy and Surrounded by Rings and Moons

Saturn is the second largest planet in our solar system. It is a ball of gas, with a cloudy atmosphere. Saturn is surrounded by thick rings of ice and rock. It has about sixty moons. A space probe has been orbiting Saturn since 2004, sending images to Earth.

Planet Fact

Saturn is sometimes called the butterscotch planet because of its yellowish color. This color is caused by haze and white clouds that lie above its atmosphere. They also make the planet appear smoother than it really is.

Saturn Looks Yellow

Because Saturn is made up of gases, it does not have an outer crust. From the outside, Saturn has a buttery yellow color. This color does not come from its surface. It comes from the Sun's light, which is reflected by the ammonia and ice clouds in the atmosphere.

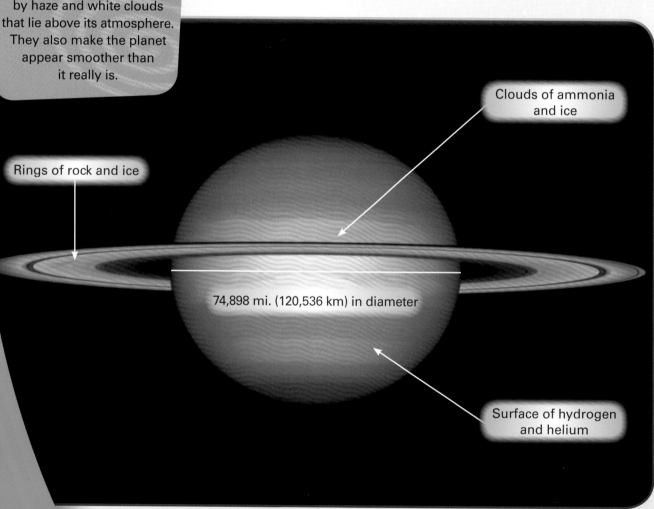

Clouds of ammonia and ice

Rings of rock and ice

74,898 mi. (120,536 km) in diameter

Surface of hydrogen and helium

 With the human eye, Saturn looks like a bright star. A telescope is needed to see its rings.

Saturn's Atmosphere Is Made of Three Layers

Saturn's atmosphere has three layers of clouds. These clouds are made of ammonia and ice. The atmosphere is very windy and there are often storms.

Saturn Is Surrounded by Rings

Saturn's rings are very bright and can be seen through a home telescope. They are made of icy lumps of dust and rock. Some of these lumps are tiny, while others are several feet across.

Saturn Is Surrounded by Many Moons

Saturn's sixty moons range in size from less than a mile to thousands of miles wide. Titan is the largest, and it is the second-biggest moon in our solar system. Jupiter's moon Ganymede is the only one larger. Titan is bigger than the planet Mercury.

FAMOUS SKY WATCHERS

In 1655, the Dutch astronomer Christiaan Huygens was the first astronomer to realize that Saturn had rings. He also discovered one of its moons, Titan.

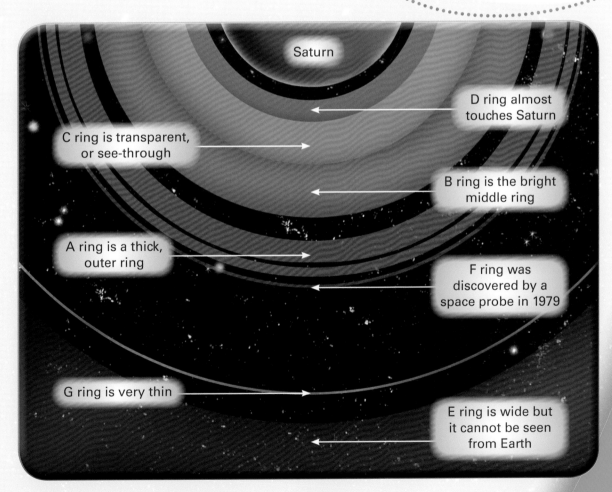

Saturn

D ring almost touches Saturn

C ring is transparent, or see-through

B ring is the bright middle ring

A ring is a thick, outer ring

F ring was discovered by a space probe in 1979

G ring is very thin

E ring is wide but it cannot be seen from Earth

Saturn has at least seven rings. Four of these can be seen from Earth with a telescope.

Uranus Is Surrounded by Rings and Moons

Uranus cannot be seen from Earth without a telescope. Little was known about this planet until a space probe flew past it in 1986. Like other gas giants, the surface and atmosphere of Uranus is made up of helium, hydrogen, and methane gases. Methane gives Uranus its blue color.

Uranus Is Surrounded by Rings

Uranus has thirteen rings that are made of rock and dust orbiting its equator. Because Uranus is tilted on its side, we see the rings running from the top to the bottom, rather than around the middle.

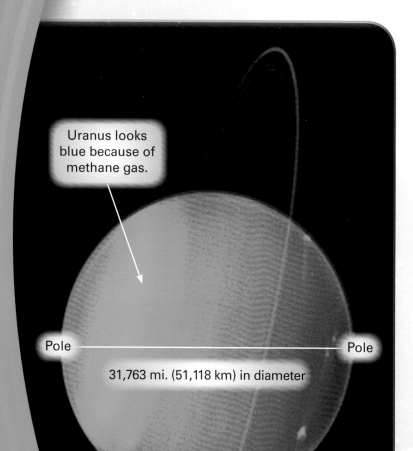

Uranus looks blue because of methane gas.

Pole

Pole

31,763 mi. (51,118 km) in diameter

Rings of rock and dust

Uranus Is Surrounded by Many Moons

Uranus has twenty-seven moons. The moons closest to Uranus orbit in the opposite direction of those farther away.

◄ Not all of Uranus's rings are clearly visible through a telescope from Earth, but they can be seen in this infrared image.

FAMOUS SKY WATCHERS

The German-British **astronomer** William Herschel discovered Uranus in 1781. At first he thought what he saw was a comet or a star. However, after observing it for some time, he realized it was a planet.

Neptune Is Cloudy and Surrounded by Rings and Moons

Neptune looks like a tiny dot when seen through a telescope from Earth. A space probe flew past the planet in 1989 and sent back images of its clouds, rings, and moons. Scientists think that Neptune is a lot like Uranus, except that it has more wind and storms.

Neptune looks blue because of methane gas.

Methane clouds

30,775 mi. (49,528 km) in diameter

Rings of fine dust

▲ Neptune looks bluer than Uranus because it has more methane gas in its atmosphere.

Planet Fact

Neptune is the outermost planet in the solar system. It is thirty times farther from the Sun than Earth. Neptune was not discovered until 1846. It can only be seen clearly through powerful telescopes.

Neptune Is Surrounded by Rings

Neptune is surrounded by five thin rings. Scientists believe they are made from fine dust from Neptune's moons.

Neptune Is Surrounded by Many Moons

Neptune has thirteen moons. Four of these sit within Neptune's rings. One of the moons is almost as large as Earth's moon, but most are quite small.

DO THE PLANETS MOVE?

From Earth, we see the planets change their positions in the night sky. This is because they are orbiting the Sun. Each one of the planets also **rotates** on its **axis**.

The Planets Orbit the Sun

In our solar system, each planet orbits the Sun at a different distance and at a different speed. For example, Earth travels around the Sun at 66,661 mi. (107,280 km) per hour. Neptune, which is much farther away, travels at only 12,147 mi. (19,548 km) per hour.

Planet Fact

It takes 224 Earth days for Venus to orbit the Sun (which equals one Venus year). It takes 243 Earth days for it to rotate on its axis. This means that a Venus day is longer than a Venus year!

How the Planets Orbit the Sun			
Planet	**Average Distance from the Sun in mi. (km)**	**Speed of Orbit in mi. (km) per hour**	**Time it Takes to Rotate 360°**
Mercury	35,983,606 (57,910,000)	107,149 (172,440)	58.6 days
Venus	67,232,363 (108,200,000)	78,293 (126,000)	243 days
Earth	92,957,130 (149,600,000)	66,661 (107,280)	23 hours 56 minutes
Mars	141,635,350 (227,940,000)	53,910 (86,760)	24 hours 37 minutes
Jupiter	483,613,199 (778,300,000)	29,304 (47,160)	9 hours 56 minutes
Saturn	888,187,982 (1,429,400,000)	21,698 (34,920)	10 hours 40 minutes
Uranus	1,783,950,479 (2,870,990,000)	15,211 (24,480)	17 hours 14 minutes
Neptune	2,798,842,261 (4,504,300,000)	12,147 (19,548)	16 hours 7 minutes

Planets that are closer to the Sun move more quickly through space than those farther away.

The Planets Rotate

Each of the planets in our solar system rotates on its axis. One whole spin equals one whole day on that planet. A day on Jupiter is the shortest, at only 9 hours 56 minutes in Earth time. A day on Venus is the longest, at 243 Earth days.

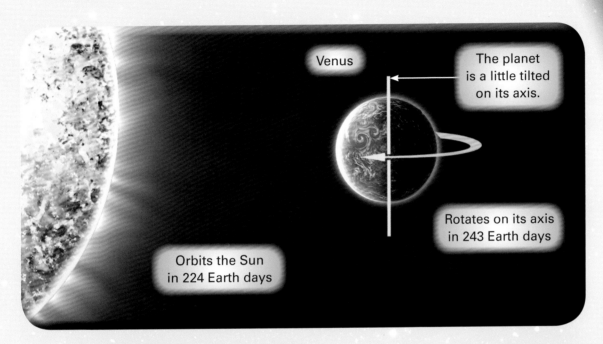

Venus

The planet is a little tilted on its axis.

Rotates on its axis in 243 Earth days

Orbits the Sun in 224 Earth days

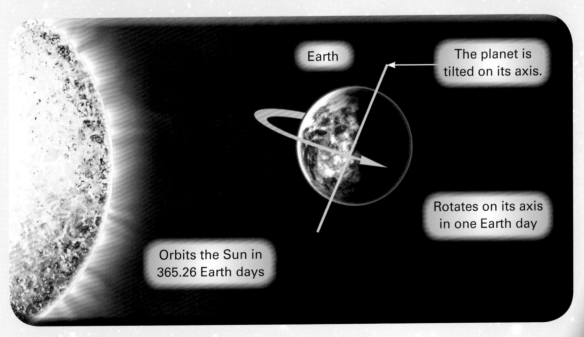

Earth

The planet is tilted on its axis.

Rotates on its axis in one Earth day

Orbits the Sun in 365.26 Earth days

∧ Venus rotates very slowly compared to Earth. It spins in the opposite direction of most planets.

HOW DO THE PLANETS AFFECT EARTH?

The other planets in our solar system affect Earth by protecting it from space object impacts. They are also Earth's neighbors in space, and people are able to learn from watching and studying the planets.

V Without the other planets, Earth may not have survived orbiting the Sun.

Planet Jupiter protects Earth from space object impacts.

Earth is a planet in the solar system, and we can learn a lot from studying the other planets.

Jupiter Protects Earth

Of all the planets, Jupiter plays the biggest part in protecting Earth. Jupiter is the largest planet and has very strong gravity. Jupiter's gravity pulls comets and asteroids toward it and away from Earth. Thousands of space objects hit Jupiter every year.

Earth Is a Planet in the Solar System

People have always watched the planets. Like stars, planets have been an important part of the night sky. For thousands of years, astronomers thought that Earth was at the center of everything. It took a long time to discover that Earth was also a planet.

Learning from the Planets

Scientists have learned a lot from studying the planets. Venus and Mars are planets that are a lot like Earth. If Earth's atmosphere becomes too polluted, it could become like Venus, which is too harsh and hot for life.

V Space probes have gathered information about all of the planets in our solar system. In 2003, the European Space Agency's *Mars Express* journeyed to Mars.

Planet Fact

Some scientists believe that Jupiter may be harmful to Earth. They believe that Jupiter's gravity pulls many space objects from the **Main Belt** and throws them into the paths of other planets.

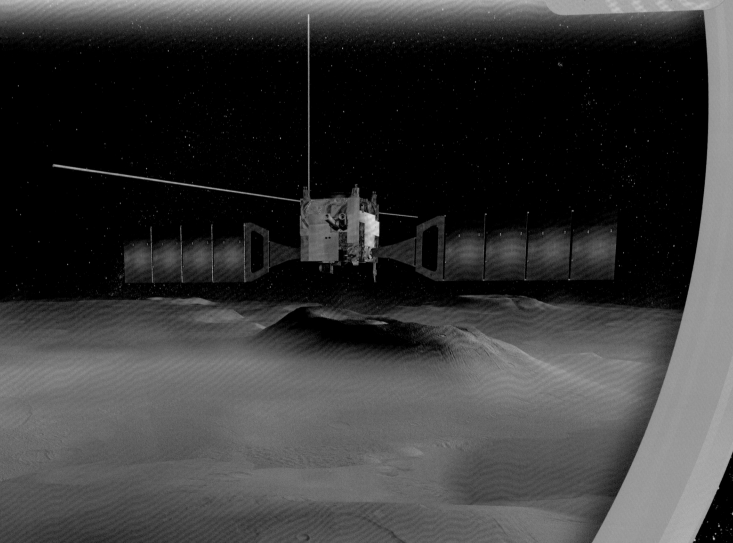

WHAT DOES THE FUTURE HOLD FOR THE PLANETS?

There are no real threats to the planets that scientists know about. Although the planets can be hit by space objects, they are not likely to be destroyed by them. It is most likely that the planets will orbit the Sun until it begins to die. At that point, the solar system will also come to an end.

Planet Fact

Scientists believe that a large space object crashed into Earth about 65 million years ago. They believe that this is what led to the death of the dinosaurs and many other living things that existed on Earth at the time.

The Planets Are Harmed by Space Objects

It is unlikely that space objects will destroy any of the planets in our solar system. However, this does not mean that space objects are not harmful. If a space object hit Earth, it could affect life on our planet badly. Large impacts throw dust into the atmosphere, blocking the Sun. Without sunlight, plants cannot grow. Without plants there is no food for animals and humans.

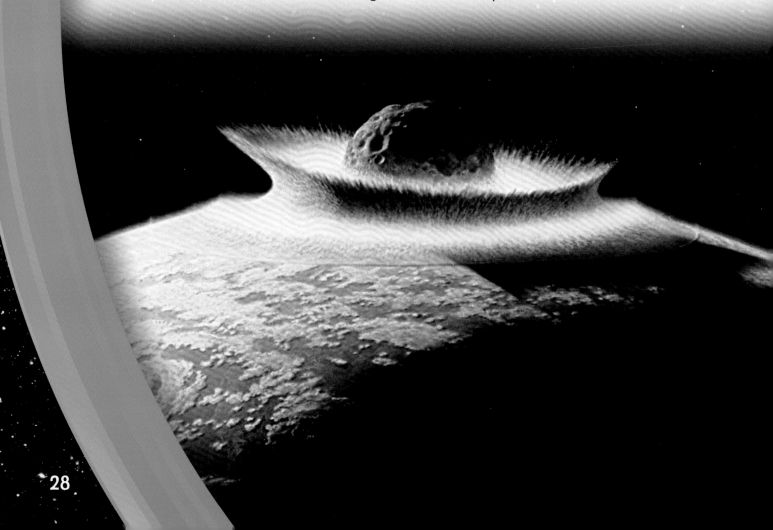

V Scientist believe that large space object impacts have caused a lot of damage on Earth in the past.

The End of the Solar System

In about 5 billion years, the Sun will become a **red giant** star. It will become about eight times larger than it is today. When this happens, the inner planets will be destroyed by its heat. The outer planets will move farther out into space. The red giant will slowly burn out to become a **white dwarf** star. At this point it will no longer have the gravity to hold the planets in orbit around it.

1. This is the solar system today.

3. The Sun will slowly become a white dwarf, losing most of its gravity. The last of the planets will drift off into space.

2. In 5 billion years, the Sun will become a red giant, burning up Mercury, Venus, and Earth. The other planets will move farther away from the Sun.

∧ Scientists believe that the planets will not die until the Sun dies billions of years from now.

FAMOUS SKY WATCHERS

Astronomers such as Paul Eddington realized that the stars produce their own energy. Knowing this, scientists figured out that stars such as our Sun have a lifespan of about 10 billion years.

WHAT IS THE BEST WAY TO PLANET-WATCH?

Planets in our solar system can be difficult to find from Earth. They do not appear at the same time or in the same place in the sky every night. Venus and Mars are the two planets that are easiest to watch. See if you can find them.

Watching Venus

Venus can be seen either in the early morning in the eastern sky, or in the early evening in the western sky. It is the brightest object in the night sky after the Moon. It is often called the morning star or the evening star.

Watching Mars

Mars is often only seen for a few months each year. It is larger than most stars and it looks red in the night sky. It comes close to Earth every twenty-six months.

Useful Equipment for Backyard Astronomy	
Equipment	**What It Is Used for**
Binoculars or a Telescope	A pair of binoculars or a telescope will help you see the planets in more detail.
Sky Chart	A sky chart will help you to identify the planets you can see in the sky. Remember these change from month to month, so make sure you have an up-to-date chart.
Compass	A compass will help you face the right direction when reading a sky chart.
Flashlight with Red Cellophane over the Lightbulb	Use a flashlight to help you read the sky chart. Putting red cellophane over the lightbulb end of the flashlight will prevent its light from affecting your night vision.

Useful Websites

Solar System: http://science.nationalgeographic.com/science/space/solar-system

Solar System: www.kidsastronomy.com/solar_system.htm

The Nine Planets: www.nineplanets.org

Welcome to the Planets: http://pds.jpl.nasa.gov/planets

Glossary

ammonia   An airlike substance that is colorless, poisonous, and has a strong smell.

asteroids   Small, rocky, or metal space objects that orbit the Sun.

atmosphere   The layer of gases that surrounds a planet, moon, or star.

axis   An imaginary line through the middle of an object, from top to bottom.

comets   Small, rocky, and icy space objects that have long, shining tails that are visible when orbiting near the Sun.

core   The center of a star, planet, or moon.

craters   Deep, round holes made by space object impacts.

crust   The outside layer of a planet or moon.

equator   An imaginary line around the middle or widest part of a round space object, such as a star or planet.

gas   A substance that is not solid or liquid, and is usually invisible.

gravitational pull   The forces of gravity that attract two objects toward each other.

gravity   The force that attracts all objects toward each other.

helium   An air-like substance that is colorless and odorless; it is the second most common gas in the universe.

highlands   Land that is hilly and higher than seas or plains, but is not as high as mountains.

hydrogen   An air-like substance that is colorless, odorless, and can easily catch on fire; it is the most common gas in the universe.

lava   Hot, liquid rock that flows out of volcanoes.

Main Belt   An area between Mars and Jupiter where thousands of asteroids and meteoroids orbit the Sun.

mantle   The middle layer of a planet or moon, between the crust and the core.

meteoroids   Small space objects that are made of rock and metal, and range from several feet wide to the size of a pea.

methane   An air-like substance that is colorless, odorless, and can easily catch on fire.

nebula   A cloud of gas and dust in space.

orbit   To travel around another, larger space object.

particles   Very small parts of substances or matter.

plains   Low-lying, flat areas of land.

radar   An instrument that uses radio waves to find the location, distance, direction, or speed of moving and fixed objects, and is often used to produce images.

red giant   A very large, cooling star.

rotates   Turns or spins around a fixed point or an axis, like a spinning top.

solar system   The Sun and everything that orbits it, including planets and other space objects.

space   The area in which the solar system, stars, and galaxies exist, also known as the universe.

white dwarf   A small, dense star that is slowly fading.

INDEX